T0303169

Parish Faith Formation Assessment and Planning Tool

Catholic Education Ministries
Diocese of St. Cloud

Jeffrey Kaster, Editor
Janet M. Peterson-Haarman
Ann Marie Biermaier, OSB
Jeff Fromm

Sheed & Ward
Franklin, Wisconsin

As an apostolate of the Priests of the Sacred Heart, a Catholic religious order,
the mission of Sheed & Ward is to publish books of contemporary impact
and enduring merit in Catholic Christian thought and action.
The books published, however, reflect the opinion of their authors and
are not meant to represent the official position of the Priests of the Sacred Heart.

Copyright © 1999 Catholic Education Ministries, Diocese of St. Cloud
Published by Sheed & Ward
7373 South Lovers Lane Road
Franklin, Wisconsin 53132
1-800-558-0580

Cover and interior design by Scott Wannemuehler

All rights reserved. No part of this book may be reproduced,
stored in a retrieval system, or transmitted, in any form or by any means,
electronic, mechanical, photocopying, recording, or otherwise,
without the written permission of Sheed & Ward.

Printed in the United States of America

Library of Congress Cataloging-in-Publication Data

Parish faith formation assessment and planning tool: Catholic
Education Ministries / Jeffrey Kaster, editor.
p. cm.
Text written by J. Kaster and others.
ISBN 1-58051-057-4 (pbk.)
1. Church renewal—Catholic Church. I. Kaster, Jeffrey.
BX1746.P2625 1999
268'.82—dc21 98-33291
CIP

Table Of Contents

Introduction

In a collaborative mode, all the faithful of the parish are encouraged to regularly assess the faith formation of their parish. The following Parish Faith Formation Assessment and Planning Tool is a voluntary process designed to help the Parish Pastoral Council or other parish leadership in its faith formation visioning, assessing, and planning.

This Faith Formation Assessment and Long Range Planning Tool addresses the various components that affect the strength of parish faith formation. This tool will help the parish vision ways of continually forming all parishioners into mature Catholic Christians while helping to accomplish the fundamental tasks of catechesis:

- Promoting knowledge of faith
- Liturgical education
- Moral formation
- Teaching to pray
- Education for Community Life
- Missionary initiation

(*General Directory For Catechesis,* 1997, #85-86).

Attention is given to the four dimensions of parish faith formation:

1) making the Word living and active for every parishioner;
2) uniting the parish in worship;
3) building community within and outside the parish;
4) serving one another and the world community.

The goals of this Parish Faith Formation and Long Range Planning Process are to:

1) assess current efforts in faith formation;
2) affirm what is good;
3) challenge the parish to address ways to improve;
4) develop a five year faith formation plan;
5) recognize diversity in parish size, makeup and location;
6) not overwhelm the parish with more work, but help parish leadership to vision one or two plans for improvement in faith formation per year;
7) communicate the results of this process with the whole parish.

Faith Formation is essential to the life of the church in that it "continues the mission of Jesus" (*National Catechetical Directory: Sharing the Light of Faith*, #32). May God continue to bless your parish and your efforts of Faith Formation.

Overview of Process

The committee may choose to complete section B before section A.

Section A: Goals. A committee with input from parishioners completes the following for each of the four faith formation goals and objectives.

1. Identify the good things already happening.
2. Reflect on ways to improve.
3. List specific plans for improvement.

Section B: Administration. The committee reviews parish administration as it relates to faith formation.

1. Complete administration sections 1-8. (Mission, goals, personnel, etc...)
2. List specific plans for improvement within administration.

Section C: Prioritize plans for improvement from Sections A & B.

Section D: Write the five year plan.

Steps to Complete Process

Step 1: **Formation of Assessment Committee.**
The parish pastoral council or committee of the council is the recommended body to complete this tool.

Step 2: **Read and review the document as a committee.**

Step 3: **Decide to begin assessment with either Section A or B.**

Step 4: **Develop a plan for getting parish input for the Goals in Section A.**
Completing Section A will work best if input is gathered from all of the following: youth, young adults, adults, senior citizens, single people, city and rural representatives (if applicable), families (with and without children), people with special needs, parish staff, parish education board, and other parish boards and organizations.

Option 1: Create your own plan.

Option 2: One pilot site had a parish supper and meeting. Parishioners were able to choose one of the goals about which to give input. Special care was taken to make sure each group had diverse representation.

Option 3: Another pilot site had the Assessment Committee work through the tool first; then committee members received input from each of the ten parish neighborhood groups.

Step 5: **Complete Sections A , B, & C.**

Step 6: **Outside consultation recommended.**
We recommend after completing Section C (Prioritized Plans), and before starting Section D (Five Year Plan), that outside consultation review your work and give input and feedback. Consultants could include diocesan education personnel, college education/theology personnel, or other religious education or planning specialists.

Step 7: **Complete Section D: Five Year Plan.**

Step 8: **Communicate Plan with Parish Community.**

Step 9: **Yearly Review and Evaluation of Five Year Plan.**

Section A: Goals

Goal 1: Word

The ministry of The Word takes many different forms...it includes proclamation and teaching (NCD, #31).

Objectives: The parish community will be able to:

1. Help people reflect on their relationship with God throughout their lives;
2. Strive for religious knowledge among the entire parish community;
3. Respect the faith development and experiences of each person.

A. Identify the good things happening in the parish to support this goal. Please list them.

B. Reflect on and dialogue about ways to improve on this goal. Possible reflection questions you might use to help you in this process are on the next page.

C. List specific plans for improvement.

Goal 1: Word Reflection Questions

Objective 1: **The parish community will be able to help people reflect on their relationship with God throughout their lives.**

- How does the parish sponsor times of reflection, retreats, missions and the Sacrament of Reconciliation for all ages?
- During times of crisis, grief, or loss for parishioners, how does the parish provide or refer parishioners to peer support groups, e.g., A.A., Beginning Experience, Retrouvaille, etc.?
- How do the faith formation programs encourage participants to reflect on their relationship with God? What is working best in this area?

Objective 2: **Parishioners will be able to strive for religious knowledge among the entire parish community.**

- How do you use the principles as outlined in the *National Catechetical Directory* in making decisions regarding appropriate content and methods of instruction for each age level and special needs groups?
- What specific educational outcomes do you have for the age levels listed? 0-5; 6-11; 12-15; 16-20; 21-40; 41-65; 66-85; 86+
- How do you assess the individual understanding of content appropriate for each one's age level? How do you use the assessment for improving student understanding?
- How do you use outside resources, diocesan personnel, e.g. media, catechist training, leadership development, in your faith formation activities?

Objective 3: **The parish community will be able to respect the faith development and experiences of each person.**

- How does the parish encourage the faith sharing and growth of its members?
- How does the parish support non-judgmental attitudes about people and faith and encourage respect for diversity, e.g., age, other religions, gender, race, ethnicity, sexual orientation, family structures, etc.?
- What do those involved in faith formation understand about the theories of developmental faith formation?

Goal 2: Worship

Worship sanctifies through prayer and sacrament (NCD, #32).

Objective: The parish community will be able to:

1. Understand, appreciate, and participate meaningfully in liturgy and prayer.

A. Identify the good things happening in the parish to support this goal. Please list them.

B. Reflect on and dialogue about ways to improve on this goal. Possible reflection questions you might use to help you in this process are on the next page.

C. List specific plans for improvement.

Goal 2: Worship Reflection Questions

Objective 1: The parish community will be able to understand, appreciate, and participate meaningfully in liturgy and worship.

- How does the parish provide creative, meaningful prayer and worship experiences?
- How is the parish integrating liturgy and faith formation?
- What opportunities for education, formation and appreciation of liturgy are provided for people of all ages, appropriate for their level of understanding, e.g., sacramental theology, RCIA, prayer, Liturgy of the Hours?
- How do you empower people to plan and participate in liturgical and prayer celebrations, e.g., liturgy formation, printed resources, liturgy committee, and involvement in liturgical ministries?

Goal 3: Community

[Faith Formation]... is a constant and concerted pastoral activity of the Christian community (NCD, #32).

Objectives: The parish community will be able to:

1. Practice a spirit of hospitality and outreach;
2. Encourage a partnership in carrying out the parish mission.

A. Identify the good things happening in the parish to support this goal. Please list them.

B. Reflect on and dialogue about ways to improve on this goal. Possible reflection questions you might use to help you in this process are on the next page.

C. List specific plans for improvement.

Goal 3: Community Reflection Questions

Objective 1: The parish community will be able to witness a spirit of hospitality and outreach.

- How are new members welcomed into your parish community, e.g., welcoming committee, newcomers' activities, follow-up after parish registration?
- How is the parish accessible and welcoming to persons with disabilities, e.g., physical accessibility to buildings and the sanctuary, sign interpreters for liturgy and faith formation sessions, liturgical roles for persons with disabilities, large print or Braille missalettes?
- How are inactive members welcomed into the parish community, e.g., inquiry sessions, RCIA, evangelization committee, parish visitations?
- How does the parish reach out to people who are poor, hungry, homeless, alienated, abused, and grieving?

Objective 2: The parish community will be able to encourage a partnership in carrying out the parish mission.

- How have parish leadership and parishioners worked together to develop a parish mission statement, goals, objectives, and action steps?
- How do parish organizations and committees publicize the mission statement, their relationship to it and collaboration with it?
- How do goals and objectives of the various parish organizations and committees relate to the parish mission and goals?
- How has the parish engaged families in a partnership for faith formation (with an awareness and respect for the diversity of family structures)?
- How does the parish sponsor mentoring relationships, e.g., marriage preparation, confirmation, RCIA, family to family, etc.?

Goal 4: Service

Service is linked to efforts to achieve social justice (NCD, #32).

Objective: The parish community will be able to:

1. Integrate Christian service and social justice throughout faith formation.

A. Identify the good things happening in the parish to support this goal. Please list them.

B. Reflect on and dialogue about ways to improve on this goal. Possible reflection questions you might use to help you in this process are on the next page.

C. List specific plans for improvement.

Goal 4: Service Reflection Questions

Objective 1: **The parish community will be able to integrate Christian service and social justice throughout faith formation.**

- How does the parish raise awareness of service needs in parish, community and world, e.g., social justice committee, printed materials, speakers, faith formation programs?

- How does the parish educate, form and support people to live a life based on Gospel values and the teaching of the social documents of the Church?

- How is service integrated at all age levels in parish faith formation:

  PARISH: funeral hospitality, soup kitchen, home health care, catechists, liturgical ministries . . .

  COMMUNITY: food shelf, housing for the homeless, Bishop's Campaign for Human Development, housing for domestic violence victims, United Way . . .

  WORLD: natural disasters, Catholic Relief Services, Bread for the World, Oxfam World Hunger . . .

Section B: Administration

To grow effectively toward the goals explored in Section A, it is important to review the administrative supports that exist in your parish. Please collate all completed administrative data into a folder.

1. Parish Mission & Goals:

	Completed	Work in process	Not Completed
A. Written Parish Mission Statement:			
B. Written Parish Goals:			

C. Who developed the parish mission statement and the parish goals and how are they communicated to the whole parish?

2. Parish Pastoral Council:

A. Does the parish have a Pastoral Council?

B. When was the constitution for the Pastoral Council last reviewed or updated?

3. Faith Formation Mission, Philosophy, Goals, Objectives, Action Plans, & Evaluations:

There are a variety of structural forms for parish faith formation. For each faith formation structure existing in the parish, please complete the following section. Examples of structures include, but are not limited to: School, Religious Education, Youth Ministry, Young Adult, Adult Education, Family Faith Formation, Lectionary Based, RCIA Based, or Small Faith Communities.

	Completed	Work in process	Not Completed
A. Name of Structure:____________________			
1. Mission Statement:			
2. Philosophy:			
3. Goals:			
4. Objectives:			
5. Action Plans:			
6. Evaluations:			
B. Name of Structure:____________________			
1. Mission Statement:			
2. Philosophy:			
3. Goals:			
4. Objectives:			
5. Action Plans:			
6. Evaluations:			

	Completed	Work in process	Not Completed
C. Name of Structure:________________			
1. Mission Statement:			
2. Philosophy:			
3. Goals:			
4. Objectives:			
5. Action Plans:			
6. Evaluations:			
D. Name of Structure:________________			
1. Mission Statement:			
2. Philosophy:			
3. Goals:			
4. Objectives:			
5. Action Plans:			
6. Evaluations:			
E. Name of Structure:________________			
1. Mission Statement:			
2. Philosophy:			
3. Goals:			
4. Objectives:			
5. Action Plans:			
6. Evaluations:			
F. Name of Structure:________________			
1. Mission Statement:			
2. Philosophy:			
3. Goals:			
4. Objectives:			
5. Action Plans:			
6. Evaluations:			

G. Reflection Questions:

1. How do the goals and objectives of the various structures relate to the Parish Mission & Goals?

2. What are areas for improvement in this section of Parish Administration?

4. Personnel:

For each parish paid or volunteer staff member, please complete the following form. Parish paid staff could include, but are not limited to: Pastor, Associate Pastor, School Principal, Religious Education Coordinator/Director, Youth Ministry Coordinator, Liturgy/RCIA Coordinator, Pastoral Associate, Parish Administrator, Maintenance, Secretary. Volunteer staff could include, but are not limited to: Religious Education Coordinator/Director, Youth Ministry Coordinator, Liturgy/RCIA Coordinator, Pastoral Associate, Parish Administrator, Maintenance, Secretary. Please include in the folder this form, the written job description, and the written yearly goals (if available).

A. Title: ______________________ ☐ Parish Paid Staff ☐ Volunteer Staff

	Completed	Work in process	Not Completed
1. Written Job Description: Comments:			
2. Written Yearly Goals: Comments:			
3. Contract: Comments:			
4. Yearly Evaluations: Comments:			

5. Supervision:
   A. Does this position have a supervisor?

   B. Does this staff position meet regularly with his/her supervisor?

6. Submits & Administers Yearly Budget: ☐ Yes ☐ No
   Comments:

7. Continuing Education:
   A. Is money budgeted for continuing education for this staff person?

   B. Please list the continuing education opportunities this staff person has participated in within the last two years.

8. Wages: Are the wages and benefits just and/or in line with diocesan guidelines?

5. Finance: Please answer the following questions.

_____ A. Does the parish have a Finance Council in place?
_____ B. Does the parish publish a yearly Financial Report?
_____ C. Do the various parish faith formation structures submit budgets for approval?
1. To whom do they submit the budget?
2. When are the budgets approved?

_____ D. Are the various parish faith formation structures responsible for administering their budgets?
_____ E. What percentage of parish income is donated to the poor, homeless, or hungry of the community or the world?
_____ F. Has the parish done any long range financial planning? If so, what?

6. Physical Accessibility for persons with disabilities: Contact Catholic Education Ministries, Diocese of St. Cloud, for a more comprehensive survey.

7. Miscellaneous Administrative Concerns:

_____ A. Does the Parish Staff have regular staff meetings? How often?
_____ B. Does the Parish Staff attend an annual or semi-annual retreat?
C. Physical Facilities:
_____ 1. Are they safe?
_____ 2. Accessible to persons with disabilities?
_____ 3. Comfortable/aesthetically pleasing?
_____ 4. Well maintained, ventilated, lit, etc...
_____ 5. Is there adequate space for faith formation programs in the parish?
_____ 6. Is there a parish long-range plan for upkeep?

D. Instructional Material and Resources:
_____ 1. Are the Religion texts used recommended by the Diocesan Office?
_____ 2. Is there adequate A.V. equipment available?
_____ 3. Does the parish bring in outside resources like speakers, films, books, etc...

E. Public Relations and Communication: Please list the ways the parish is successful in these areas:

F. Long Range Planning: What plans has the parish made for the next five years?

8. Plans for Administrative Improvement

After completing Section B 1-7: Administration, list specific plans for improvement in this area.

A.

B.

C.

SECTION C: PRIORITIZED PLANS FOR IMPROVEMENT

Directions:

Review the plans for improvement for each goal in Section A (pp. 7, 9, 11, & 13) and for the Administration Section (p.20). Prioritize the top three specific plans for improvement in each area and write them below. This will produce a summary of the prioritized plans for improvement.

Goal 1: Word

1.

2.

3.

Goal 2: Worship

1.

2.

3.

Goal 3: Community

1.

2.

3.

Goal 4: Service

1.

2.

3.

Administration

1.

2.

3.

SECTION D: FIVE YEAR FAITH FORMATION PLAN

Directions:

After completing Section C: Prioritized Plans for Improvement, choose one to two plans for improvement per year that you can commit to work on within five years. We recommend that you limit the number of plans in any one year, so that you do not overwhelm the parish with work. For each plan, list the person responsible to initiate it, the budget, if any, and the timeline.

Parish:________________ **City:**________________ **Date:**____________

	Person(s) Responsible	Budget	Timeline
Year 1:________			
Plan 1			
Plan 2			
Year 2:________			
Plan 1			
Plan 2			
Year 3:________			
Plan 1			
Plan 2			
Year 4:________			
Plan 1			
Plan 2			
Year 5:________			
Plan 1			
Plan 2			

History

The Faith Formation Assessment and Planning Tool was developed over a five year period. It began with the establishment of faith formation goals by a St. Cloud Diocesan Religious Education Curriculum Committee in 1990. A new committee was then formed with the task to develop an assessment and planning tool for parishes. This St. Cloud Diocesan Faith Formation Assessment Committee was comprised of parish, diocesan, and college personnel representing Catholic schools, religious education, youth ministry, and persons with disabilities. Four years were then spent drafting, re-drafting, consulting, piloting, evaluating, and then finalizing this Faith Formation Assessment and Planning Tool. What follows is a brief history of the development of this tool.

1990 Diocesan Religious Education Curriculum Committee publishes seven diocesan goals. Catholic Education Ministries, Diocese of St. Cloud, conducts listening sessions which reveal need for parish faith formation assessment tool. Development of a parish faith formation assessment tool is included in Catholic Education Ministries Five Year Plan: 1991-1996.

1991 Diocesan Faith Formation Assessment Committee is formed representing: Catholic Schools, Religious Education, Youth Ministry, Persons with Disabilities, the diocese, and Education Department of College of St. Benedict/St. John's University.

1992 First Draft is completed in Fall. Received input from Bishop Jerome Hanus, OSB, the Diocesan Chair of Personnel and Planning, and a newly ordained priest.

1993 Second draft is written in January. Bishop Jerome Hanus recommends getting input from rural perspective. Three parishes in the St. Cloud Diocese pilot process: Fergus Falls, Becker, and St. Joseph.

1994 Further input is given from Pat Forster, OSF, Associate Director, Office of Research and Planning, Archdiocese of Chicago. Sites complete pilot process & formal evaluation. The pilot sites were unanimous in recommending to simplify the tool. The original seven goals were incorporated as objectives into the current four faith formation goals in Section A.

1995 Final draft of Parish Faith Formation Assessment and Planning Tool.

1997 Received the National Catholic Catechetical Leadership Research Award April 14, 1997 at the NCCL national meeting.

Acknowledgments

Catherine Kallhoff, SSND, Director of Total Education, Diocese of St. Cloud.

Parishes that piloted the Assessment & Planning Tool: Our Lady of Victory Parish, Fergus Falls, MN; Immaculate Conception Parish, Becker, MN; St. Joseph Parish, St. Joseph, MN.

Persons who provided feedback on the Tool: Catherine Kallhoff, SSND, Director of Total Education, Diocese of St. Cloud; Bishop Jerome Hanus, OSB; Rev. Gregory Lieser, Director of Personnel and Planning, Diocese of St. Cloud; Rev. Anthony Oelrich, Co-Pastor, 5 Parish Cluster, Holdingford Area; Rev. Thomas Knoblach, Pastor, St. Ann's Parish, Wadena; Pat Forster, OSF, Associate Director, Office of Research and Planning, Chicago Archdiocese.

St. Cloud Diocesan Faith Formation Assessment Committee Members: Ann Marie Biermaier, OSB, Associate Professor of Education, College of St. Benedict/St. John's University; Joan Felling, OSB, Former Consultant for Catholic Schools, Diocese of St. Cloud; Jeff Fromm, Former Director of Religious Education, Ss. Peter and Paul Parish, Richmond, MN; Janet M. Peterson-Haarman, Consultant for Religious Education & Faith Formation, Diocese of St. Cloud; Anita Harris-Walz, Principal, Sacred Heart School, Sauk Rapids; Jeffrey Kaster, Committee Chair, Consultant for the Formation of Youth, Catholic Education Ministries, Diocese of St. Cloud; Dean Mohs, Former Youth Ministry Coordinator, Sauk Centre; Joyce Seivert, OSB, Former Consultant for Persons with Disabilities, Diocese of St. Cloud.

Principle Authors: Jeffrey Kaster, Consultant for the Formation of Youth, Catholic Education Ministries, Diocese of St. Cloud. Adjunct professor, St. John's University, Collegeville. Doctoral student in Educational Policy and Administration at the University of Minnesota. M.A. in Theology from St. John's University, Collegeville. Published *Youth Ministry*, Liturgical Press, 1989. A parish youth minister for thirteen years. Committee Chairperson and Editor.

Janet M. Peterson-Haarman, Consultant for Religious Education & Faith Formation, Catholic Education Ministries, Diocese of St. Cloud. Graduate of the College of St. Catherine, St. Paul. Graduate work in theology at St. John's University, Collegeville. A parish director of religious education for eleven years.

Ann Marie Biermaier, OSB, St. Joseph, Minnesota, teaches in the Education Department at the College of Saint Benedict and Saint John's University, St. Joseph, Minnesota. Doctor of Education degree in Educational Administration from the University of North Dakota. Previous experiences include teaching and serving as a principal in several parochial elementary schools in central Minnesota and chairing the Education Department at the College of Saint Benedict.

Jeff Fromm has been involved in church education for over 24 years. He served as a Catholic School Principal for eight years, worked with children and youth and as a Director of Faith Formation for sixteen years focusing primarily on adult and family formation. He is experienced in leading workshops for teachers and planners, has published several educational tools for teaching, and is committed to effective educational planning in the local church.